The Book of Olio

Reshma Raju Emmatty

BookLeaf Publishing

To Daddy, my storyteller. You were the coolest
grandparent, ever.

To Kevin, for holding the fort while I go chasing
one crazy endeavour after another. Thank you
for being the wind beneath my wings.

To Rufus, for the snuggles, the paw-fives and the
wet-nosed kisses. Good boy, Rufus!

To you. Yes, *you*. I'm really glad you decided to
pick up *The Book of Olio*. Really, thank you!

Preface

The Book of Olio, as the name suggests, is about a little bit of everything -sunshine, smiles, love, grief, anguish, Rufus and even an elephant who flew to the moon.

Just like its contents, the style used for each poem in this book is also distinct (except for the two free verses and the two limericks). I had fun learning about various poetic styles and applying them in *The Book of Olio*.

Three weeks of thinking, scribbling, crossing things out, re-writing, chewing on the ends of multiple pens and similar activities lead to this book. If even one of these poems can put a smile on your face, I will be one happy wordsmith.

Happy reading!

Petrichor

How like petrichor is your scent to me!
I feel your presence in winds and the rains.
In distant lands or the sea, you may be –
Earnestly I wait, though shackled in chains.

It was a blushing spring morn' we first met -
Into the night, we had so much to say.
Flowers to fall leaves, we hadn't kissed yet;
Rain was our witness, as love found its way.

For my hand, they made you bid me farewell,
Locked me up, tasked you with treasures to seek;
Caught in this scheming web for a long spell,
Only the rains I hear; I long to speak.

I *know* you will find your way to me, dear,
This rain tells me that you are nearly here.

A Starry Haiku

Blazing through the sky
Shooting stars hide from most eyes,
Making wishes true.

A Feline Limerick

There was a lady whose lips never smiled;
So had she remained since she was a child.
Then she got a cat -
Mighty change was that!
With everyone in town she reconciled.

An Ode to a (North American) Summer

Dreamy Dandelion buds raise their head
Through a verdant flourish after the snow.
Robin perches on the Oak, her wings spread;
Of warmth and sunny days, how soon they know!
With tiny paws, bushy-tailed squirrels hold
And nibble at acorns, flowers and seeds.
Little grey rabbits have now become bold
Enough to emerge from the bushy weeds.
Sunshine and shorter nights making their way,
Waking flowers to make Summer's bouquet.

There, in the creek gently swims the Mallard
By the reeds is the hen, and their ducklings.
Liquid cerulean waters lingered
Before the fall to join sister springs.
In all its glory, the early sunrise
To moonless nights adorned with astral glint,
With the first yellow leaf we realize
That time flies too fast, and wish that it didn't.
Season most cherished, most longed for all year,
Summer, you bring us exorbitant cheer.

A Troubled Tanka

Like jagged glass shards,
Unkind words pierced her heart
Over and over
Till she cried herself to sleep
just like she used to, and will.

Lift Your Sisters Up!

Lift your sisters up as you march ahead,
Hurdles are strewn all about them, you see.
Cause equality and kindness to spread.

To some, they exist only to be wed;
To others, unpaid housekeepers they be.
Lift your sisters up as you march ahead.

When young children should play and learn to read
Forced out of schools, to cook, clean and make tea!
Cause equality and kindness to spread.

"No!", "Don't" and "Cannot" – the only words said.
What *can* she do once she hits puberty?
Lift your sisters up as you march ahead.

At work, glass ceilings; a feeling of dread -
She's not given that opportunity.
Cause equality and kindness to spread.

Don't let patriarchal forces embed
Discrimination; Now, this is a plea -
Lift your sisters up as you march ahead,
Cause equality and kindness to spread.

Rufus, the Royal.

Rufus thinks he's a King;
Humans sure treat him so -
Concierge gets the door,
Mommy at beck and call,
All for this Labrador

Rufus thinks he's a King
Ruling over humans.
Always ready to play,
Wakes up each day thinking
"What can I do today?".

Rufus thinks he's a King.
Hates competition, he
Pees on hydrants and trees
Claimed by other canines -
Annexes all he sees.

Rufus thinks he's a King –
Humans bow down to him!
They crave his attention
As he gaits down the road -
Picture of perfection.

A Sunset Cinquain

Sunsets
Paint the Sky with
Colours so magical,
Stealing away our days and hearts
Each time.

An Acrostic Attempt

Ready to write an Acrostic?
Every one can. Yes, even you!
Start each line with an alphabet,
Holding the word you want to spell
Maintain them in the right sequence.
And you have it – an Acrostic!

A Light List of Things

If you have plans to visit Toronto,
Mother will get in touch with you, pronto.
Joan's neighbour's third cousin's landing tonight-
Surely, Mother has sent me something light.
How many kilos can travellers take?
I hope she's sent me her chocolate cake,
Bottles of pickles all packed nice and tight
Of Mangoes and lemons and dates, that's right!
At least one bottle of sweet home-made wine,
Tasty, whole gooseberries bottled in brine,
Thinly sliced, crispy fried banana chips
Are worth those extra pounds around my hips.
Spicy, golden brown cutlets of minced meat
Paired with a secret sauce dipping, so neat!
Creams for my face and the pills for headache,
Nutmegs for tummy ache, make no mistake.
In that suitcase she'd slip my books into
Would there be a *Balarama* or two?
What's that you say - Did they throw things away
So that Airlines let them go on their way?
No, it *can't* be…I…I need a moment.
Volunteer, visitors! End my torment.

Read Between the Lines

- A Short Echo Verse

He proposed, Oh My!
I
Don't know what to do
Do
He assures his love
Love
But, do I love him?
Him.

Now, He Flies!

He brushed his tears on his right sleeve
And quietly, he took their leave
On that saturnine Christmas eve.

To all his rebukers' surprise
He worked his way up to his prize
And soon his fame started to rise.

Now they all watch him as he flies.
Shoots at him with malice and lies
In vain; He's won in the world's eyes.

Igniting Embers

Be unapologetically yourself.
Some bask in your warmth,
Stay for your intense ardour,
And leave at the slightest singe.
Don't tame your flames
Only to please them -
They, who like you warm
but not too feisty;
They, who like to play
Hephaestus or Hestia,
Until they realize that
Fire, unlike clay, cannot be moulded.
Don't let them snuff out
your roaring, raging blaze.
That fire in you may scare some,
scathe some, and burn others.
Be nobody's fool.
Be, *Inferno*.

Thrive

Life may lead you far away from your roots-
Faraway lands, for your dreams to come true.
New tastes, new people, new words and new routes
Seize that opportunity, have no rue.

Faraway lands, for your dreams to come true.
Faraway, home; do you leave it behind?
Seize that opportunity, have no rue,
Make your peace, have tranquility of mind.

Faraway, home; do you leave it behind?
Old tastes, old people, old words and old routes…
Make your peace, have tranquility of mind -
To grow, you need both; green shoots, and deep roots.

Old tastes, old people, old words and old routes -
Never forget, as you grow new green shoots.
To grow, you need both – green shoots, and deep roots;
For, life may lead you far away from your roots.

For Her

Come not with moist eyes,
Sweet, empty words or sighs.
Her eyes are now shut tight
To every shred of light.
Save your kind sympathies
Sent from across the seas.

A shoulder to cry on,
A true friend to call on,
A love, strong, to hold on,
May have helped her stay on.
For *her* sake, be that hope,
For those reaching for a rope.

Falling for Fall

Pumpkins and Apples.
Scarlet, Gold and Amber leaves.
Fall, in russet glory.

Maple Pecan tarts
Baked with love and cinnamon,
Topped with sugar dust.

Corn maze and long hikes,
S'mores toasted at campfires,
In crispy Fall air.

Family and friends
Come together to give thanks,
Hearts and bellies full.

Jack O' Lanterns smile,
Ghouls and monsters take to streets,
For Halloween night.

Fall charms our senses
With its enchanting beauty
Till Winter's first snow.

To the Moon!

There was an Elephant and a Loon
Who wanted to fly up to the Moon.
A man from Korea
Gave them an idea...
Soon, they flew up on a big balloon!

Rant of a Millennial Woman

"What bothers you, dear? Our time starts right now…"
"Where do I begin? Since I was a child?
They loved me dearly; I can't deny that.
Toys, games and Barbie dolls, I had them all.

It started with clothes, I guess, when I grew tall,
My teacher wanted my skirt hems let down;
'Don't distract boys as you walk up the stairs' –
Were the boys asked not to look up our skirts?

'Speak softly', 'Be demure', 'Sit like a girl'
Were just a few commands thrown at us girls.
We learned to wash our plates and press our clothes –
Were the boys asked to help out at their homes?

Teen years with pimples and hormones galore
Baffled us with changes, feelings and more.
When young men stalked us or older men leered,
Why were we told that it was all our fault?

They wanted us to work hard at our schools,
Take up hobbies and bring home the trophies,
Until one day they decide we're of age-
Why did they not care about our careers?

Walks monitored, our phone calls are observed,
What we see, what we read – all that's censored.
They police us at every little turn
Are we not adults when we turn eighteen?

Elders say *this* and religion says *that*.
Decisions, pre-made for all our lives.
When it's time to face the big world out there,
How can we learn to think on our two feet?

All through our lives they say, 'Don't talk to boys'.
Now, with a stranger they want us to live!
'We had no problems', 'That's how we all met' -
How can I find *the one* over a tea?

My friend and I share our start date at work.
Why does he get preference over me?
If that's how things are when I am not wed,
How would it be when I have a baby?"

"Well, my dear, I think we are now at time…"
"Oh, but I was only getting started…"
(Reaches for a tissue for that lone tear)
"I know, my dear, I'll see you next Tuesday."